This book is dedicated to my 3 beautiful girls:
Teresa, Brooke and Brynn

Originally published 2011

Copyright 2011 by David Vyse
All rights reserved.

ISBN 978-0-9868552-0-7

MOST RELOCATED ANIMALS WILL DIE DUE TO STRESS, COMPETITION FOR SPACE OR LACK OF FOOD RESOURCES.

Whether your animal issue is in the home, under the deck or shed, or in the garden, this book will show you how the professionals handle these situations and the tools that they use.

This fully illustrated guide will give you step-by-step instructions on removing urban wildlife and building simple animal proof structures and devices aimed at keeping wildlife out. Each section will discuss a variety of circumstances to fit your own needs. Every chapter shows you how to carefully, professionally and humanely handle urban wildlife when it gets too close for comfort.

Living with urban wildlife is something that won't change. The focus of this book is not to trap and relocate wildlife – this does not solve the problem. If anything this will create more problems within your community and is inhumane to the animal. The focus is to remove urban wildlife from your home safely and effectively and prevent any future problems that may occur.

Throughout this guide, always bear in mind that animals are normally afraid of humans. We are bigger and for the most part smarter. They will not bite unless provoked or threatened, so it's best to be gentle. They just want out.

All of the information in this guide is based on what I have learned in the field of wildlife control and also in my many years of education in wildlife management. Some of the tips and techniques may not work in certain circumstances. Remember that you are dealing with wild animals which are unpredictable. I will give you the basic knowledge and tools you need, but you may have to get creative. If all else fails, call a reputable wildlife removal company.

Copyright © 2011 by David Vyse. All rights reserved. Reproduction of any part of this publication without written permission of the publisher is strictly forbidden.

CONTENTS

Getting Started 1
Determining what's up there 1
Materials used throughout this guide 4
Areas on your home vulnerable to wildlife 6

Raccoons 13
In the attic 14
In the chimney 19
Under the deck 22

Skunks 23

Squirrels 27
In the house 28
Getting to know your squirrels 30
In the attic 31

Birds 33
In the house 34
In the vents 34
In the walls 37

Bats 41
In the house 42
In the attic 44

Mice 47
In the house 48

Other nuisance wildlife 49
In the garage 50
In the yard 51

DETERMINING
what's up there

Let's start by figuring out what kind of animal you are dealing with. This is a common occurrence: you are awakened in the middle of the night by a scratching noise coming from the attic and then it stops. What was that?

Keep in mind that whatever kind of animal may be present, it will do structural damage. With mice it is minimal but with squirrels and raccoons the damage may be significant. Squirrels can chew wires, beams and drywall. Raccoons can destroy insulation and drywall by urinating and defecating. Both animals can become a major health and safety risk if not removed.

Here are some general rules of thumb to determine what kind of animal is up there and how serious the problem is.

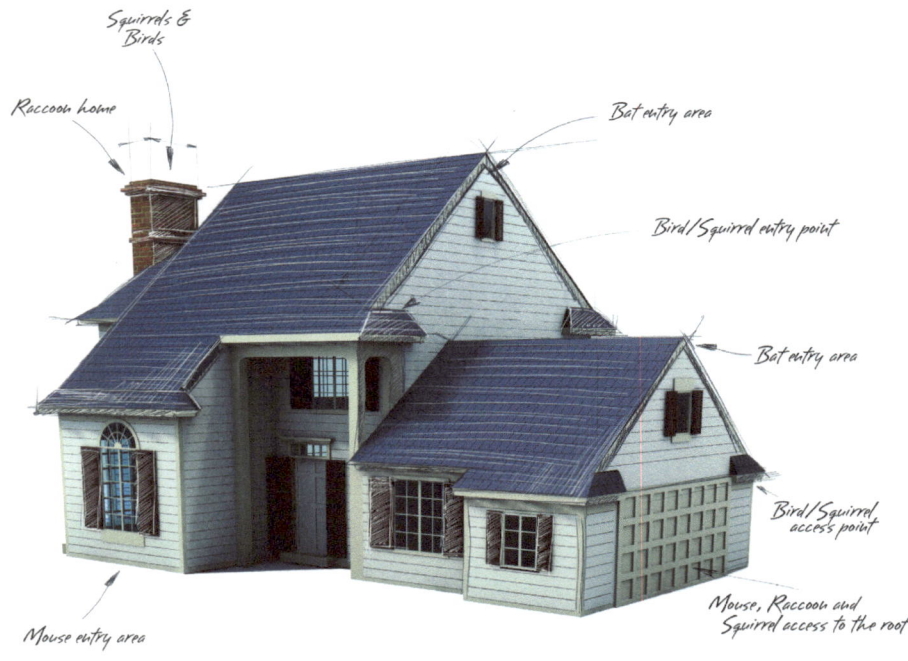

1 Getting Started

MICE are generally nocturnal (active during the night). You will hear a scratching or chewing noise in one area and it will stop and possibly start again in the same or another area. When you hear the noise, try banging on that area. If the noise stops and goes quiet, or starts back up after a minute or so, it's a mouse (refer to page 47). If you hear the animal move around or run away, you're dealing with something bigger.

Another way of determining if you are dealing with mice is to examine the attic – open the hatch and use a flashlight to look around. If you have blown insulation you will see trails which the animal will use as a corridor or pathway. Mice spend most of their time in the walls and attic and this is where you will see the most activity. If mice are present, there may be distinct small holes and trails about 2 inches in width. The trails are typically so well-used that the insulation becomes partially packed down. If the trails are wider than 2 inches or the insulation is completely packed down, you're dealing with a larger animal.

RACCOONS are generally nocturnal. Normally they move slowly in the attic, making a brushing sound when in their den but they are much louder when coming and going (it will sound like a person in your attic). If there are babies present they are very vocal and will chatter for hours during the night while the mother is out foraging for food. They sound like birds when they are young (refer to page 8).

SQUIRRELS are generally active during the day. You will hear running or moving around in the early morning and late afternoon and perhaps some activity during the day, but rarely at night. If babies are involved you may hear excessive chewing in one area at various hours of the day and night, but this will not be an every night occurrence (refer to page 11).

SKUNKS are unable to enter the attic because they cannot climb. Mostly they spend their time under structures like sheds, porches and decks (refer to page 13).

> **quick fact**
> Bat droppings will crumble if rubbed between your fingers, whereas mice droppings are more solid.

BIRDS are active early in the morning. They usually nest close to the entry area so the noises will be concentrated in one area. They love to make nests in roof vents (which are usually covered inside with window screen and accessible from the attic). This means they have not entered the attic YET but if left, the weight of the nest can break the screen, and the nest will fall into the attic leaving a family of baby birds loose in there. The baby birds will probably not be able to find their way out. This is another way squirrels and raccoons find these areas. They smell the nest and attempt to eat the eggs within the nest, thus finding an easy entry hole right into a warm area (your attic). If it is currently only birds present, fix it quickly (refer to page 33).

Birds also love to make their nests in wall vents attached to the bathroom or stove fan. Check these areas, especially if you live in a newer home. (refer to page 7)

BATS are attic intruders that most home owners are not aware of until the bats enter into the house (refer to page 41). In the warmer months of July and August, bats will exit just after dark, so take a walk around the house quietly to see if you can hear or see anything. When re-entering they will typically land on the outside wall and crawl into a space where the soffit (eaves overhang) meets the wall. Look carefully for bat droppings; they are small and black (about the size of a grain of rice) and they will be present on the ground under the entry area or stuck to the wall.

Bat droppings will crumble if rubbed between your fingers, whereas mice droppings are more solid. Bats usually enter where the soffit (overhang) meets the exterior wall. If the entry area is white or light in color you will see a dark patch where the oil from the bat's fur has rubbed off.

Materials Used

This section details specific materials and equipment needed to solve your wildlife problem, what they look like, and how they are used. Most of the materials can be found in any hardware or home improvement store and are inexpensive to buy.

1. Wire Mesh/Screen

Every application in this book requires screen (**except with mice**). Screen can often be found at hardware stores. If they do not carry the recommended screening another variation may do, depending on the animal. The rationale behind using screen is the animal can see its entry hole. In trying to get back in, it will pull and chew, focusing its energy on the screen. This will most likely stop it from destroying the rest of your roof and home. For squirrels and raccoons you want a 1" by 1" galvanized steel screening (just a bit smaller than the thickness of a coat hanger wire). It sounds thick, but that's what you will need to be successful. Anything larger than a 1" by 1" hole will allow mobile baby squirrels to fit through. For bats (if needed), you can use hardware cloth 1/2" by 1/2" or smaller but nothing less in wire strength. The reasons for using these two screens is that they are able to be bent into position easily and keep their shape, they resist rusting, and they can be cut to the appropriate size. Chicken wire is not appropriate screening as it is not strong enough.

2. Screws and Washers

These are what hold the screen in place. It is best to go to the hardware store and handpick the screws that will fit the particular job and match a washer with the screw. Be sure that the washers are larger than 1" by 1" to cover the screen squares (if you're using 1/2" screening, buy washers accordingly). I recommend using screws longer than one inch for security reasons.

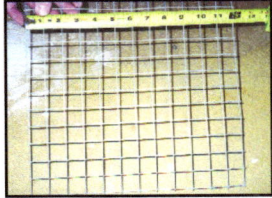

1" x 1" galvanized steel screening

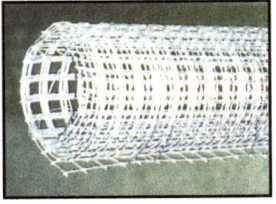

0.5" x 0.5" wire screening

3. Mini Bolt Cutters or Multi Purpose Center Cut Piano Wire Cutters

Available at most hardware stores, these are used to cut the screen to the appropriate sizes. If you are working with hardware cloth, tinsnips will do the trick.

4. A Drill (preferably cordless)

Most people already have one of these, but if not, borrow your neighbours or even better, now you have a perfect excuse to buy one! I suggest a 9 volt or higher, which is not too heavy, but has adequate power.

5. Things that you will need for the attic if you're going up

You'll need a flashlight, a stepladder to get to the hatch (depending where your hatch is), a net for poking around and a box if babies are possibly involved. Gloves and a dust mask are recommended as well because of the insulation.

6. Things that you will need if securing areas on the roof

Roof patch (or roof tar), a ladder tall enough to reach the roofline, a drill, screws and appropriate materials to complete the job.

7. Things that you will need for any animal under a structure

A shovel and an old pair of shoes.

8. Things that you will need for securing gaps

You'll need a caulking gun and caulking or silicon, depending on the size of the gap at the entry points.

There are all makes and colours of caulking. You are usually safe if you buy clear and make sure it has a 20+ year guarantee.

Also, you'll need screen for the bat exit door you will be creating and installing (hardware cloth).

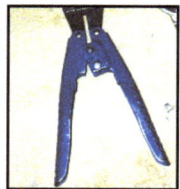
Multi-Purpose Center Cut Piano Wire Cutters

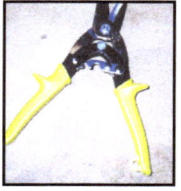
Tinsnips

Cordless Drill

Caulking Gun and Silicon

TIP: ALWAYS WEAR A MASK IN THE ATTIC TO PROTECT FROM INSULATION.

Areas on your home vulnerable to wildlife

There are a few main reasons why animals enter certain areas. One main reason is that they are attracted to ideal temperatures escaping from your home (cool in the summer and warm in the winter). Any area that allows air to leave the house can be a potential entry area for wildlife.

Urban animals are creatures of habit, so in an urban setting where most were born in an unnatural structure such as an attic or chimney, they will seek similar areas. There are several ways for an animal to access the attic, and most of the time the same animal targets the same "way in" on all the houses in the neighborhood.

TIP:

ATTACH A BUNGEE CORD TO THE TOP OF THE LADDER AND THE EAVES SO THAT THE LADDER WILL BE MORE SECURE AND NOT BLOW DOWN.

The many ways an animal can access the roof

Raccoons will use various objects such as the eaves, tv towers and vines to gain access to the roof. Squirrels are able to climb anything with a rough surface such as brick or wood.

Getting Started

HOW TO

screen
a roof vent

① **LIFT ROOF VENT TO MEASURE SIZE OF HOLE**
② **CUT SCREEN TO SIZE**
③ **SLIDE OUT SCREEN UNDER VENT**
④ **RESECURE THE VENT**

Areas on a home to check when you have an unwanted guest

ROOF VENTS: They are found on almost every home, located on the roof. They allow air to flow out of the attic. There are many styles of roof vents; some are better than others and only a few are animal proof. The best ones are made from metal (plastic may become brittle from years in the sun) and are a solid vent with no edges to grab.

Metal roof vent

If this type of roof vent is not available, (check your local hardware store) you can make it animal-proof by lifting the vent off the roof and sliding a pre-measured and pre-cut piece of screen between the vent and the roof. Make sure the hole cut in the roof under the vent leading into the attic is completely covered. Place the vent back against the roof and secure with screws and washers (don't forget the roof patch on each screw to prevent leaks).

WALL VENTS: These are areas on the home that expel air from inside with the use of a fan. They are most commonly found in the bathroom, over the stove and from the dryer. These areas mostly attract birds and sometimes squirrels. The warm air exhausted from the house attracts birds in the cooler months.

Newer subdivisions tend to have more of a problem with this – possibly because the building site was a feeding and breeding ground for the birds the previous year. The most common bird that enters a vent is the European Starling (Sturnus vulgaris) and it is definitely the most destructive. They enter by flying against the vent, wedging their beaks into the louvers and pushing them up to expose an opening, allowing access. See page 38, sealing a wall vent.

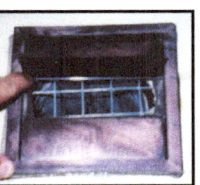
Screened Wall Vent

CHIMNEYS: One of the most common areas wildlife will enter is the chimney as it is an open hole with inviting warm or cool temperatures coming out. To remove an animal, refer to the proper chapter, but to seal this area from further invasion choose a cap that:
- has a screen that does not move
- does not "screw" into your clay liner
- has a non-movable wire cage
- has a wire going up to the steel roof of the cap with no gaps
- fits tightly where the metal meets the clay liner

ROOF / FASCIA SPACE: This is where the roof plywood meets the board that the eavestrough is nailed to (fascia board). Many times there will be a gap in this area when the house was built and it is sometimes big enough for an animal to squeeze into or chew on. One other reason for animals entering through this area is from the roof board warping in sections, exposing gaps. This area is especially susceptible to rotting because of ice buildup in the eavestrough – making the wood soft and allowing an animal to rip or chew a hole into your attic.

UNSECURE
SECURE

quick fact The only animal able to climb back out of a chimney once down is an adult raccoon, even birds cannot fly out once they've fallen into the chimney

Getting Started 8

HOW TO

screen
a gable vent
from inside the attic

   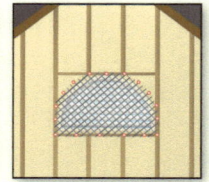

1. **MEASURE TO THE SURROUNDING JOISTS**
2. **CUT SCREEN TO SIZE**
3. **SECURE EVERY 10 INCHES AROUND PERIMETER**

Roof / Fascia Space continued...

An easy way to prevent this problem before it happens is to install drip edge. This is a metal flashing that is angled to fit up under the shingles and down the back of the eavestrough. If an animal has already violated this area you may want to install the drip edge around the rest of the house, fastening it with screws, leaving the entry area open to deal with the wildlife problem first.

Make sure to seal the entry hole with screen only. The rationale behind the screen is that the animal can see into the hole, only pulling and chewing on this area and not the rest of the house. Go to the corresponding chapter involving your specific wildlife problem.

GABLE VENTS: These are located on some homes at either end of the

No Drip edge

Drip edge

One piece gable vent with solid louvers

house's exterior peak walls near the roof. They allow air to vent out of the attic. What they are made of and how wide the louvers are will determine which animal will enter at this location. If you can find a gable vent with solid louvers that will fit, buy it, but more than likely, the best way to secure this area is with screen over the inside of the hole.

To secure it, access the vent from in the attic. Cut a piece of screen big enough to reach the inside joists around the vent (it doesn't have to be pretty, no one will see it) and screw it into the wood every 10 inches around the perimeter. This will not stop birds from nesting in the louvers, but it is by far the most esthetically pleasing method and no animal will enter the attic. If the nests are a problem, repeat the steps on the exterior of the house and keep it neat following the contours of the vent.

SOFFIT VENTS: These are found on homes with wood soffits and they complete the airflow through the attic. They are usually secured with nails and over time might become loose, allowing animals to pull or chew on the vent, gaining access.

From the ground they look impossible to get to but are easily accessible for animals. They are very easy to seal. Measure the size of the opening or existing vent and add an inch on all sides for overhang. Cut the screening to the measured size and place it over the vent and secure (you can use a staple gun to secure the screen or screws and washers but they are more visible). You should leave the old vent in place under the screen to prevent insects from getting in (it looks nicer as well). Raccoons enter mainly through these areas if left unscreened.

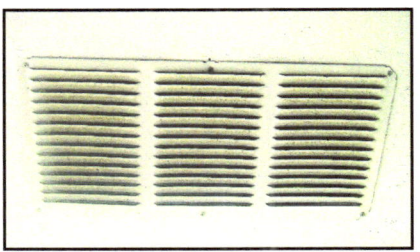

Typical Soffit Vent

> **quickfact**
> The roof soffit intersection is one of the most common areas for a raccoon to enter a home.

Getting Started 10

Roof / Soffit Intersections:

This is where the upper roof overhang meets the lower roof. It is present on backsplits, sidesplits, or areas jutting out from the house. This area is a major problem.

When a house is constructed, the builders are unable to secure this area, allowing the soffit to push up where it meets the roof. This leaves lots of room for entry right into the attic. This is a very difficult area to secure or screen and a very common access point for raccoons.

There are two options, one being to re-secure the area yourself, which means adding screws to the aluminum piece attached to the house and to the aluminum that covers the outer side of the soffit, under the eaves. The other option, which is a little more noticeable but considerably more secure, is to measure the width of

Roof/Soffit Intersections

Roof/Soffit Intersection

the soffit and cut a piece of screen big enough to make a large V. Slide it into the area attaching it to the roof and the soffit and into the wall.

Escaping from your chimney

Only adult raccoons can come and go freely from a chimney with a clay liner. All other animals will be trapped at the bottom and unable to exit once down. Raccoons are able to climb up by putting their backs against one side of the clay liner and their arms and legs to the other side and shimmying their way to the top. Even birds once at the bottom cannot manage to fly out.

HOW TO

Re-secure the roof/soffit intersection

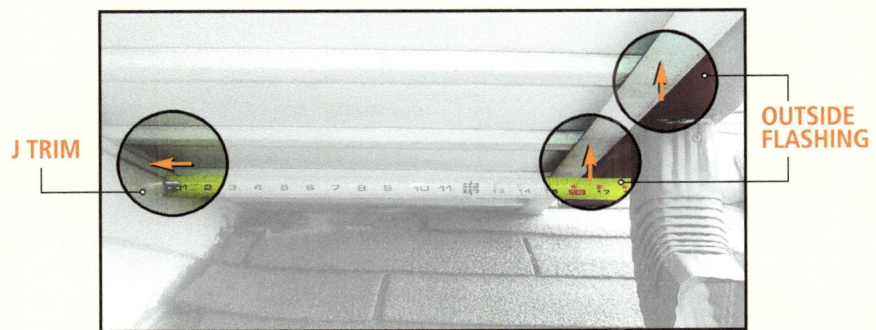

Insert screws through the J trim into the wall (the J trim holds the soffit in place along the inside wall). This will secure the area closest to the inside wall. Also screw the outside flashing that folds under the eaves up into the fascia board. The arrows show the areas that need to be secured. Once the spot where the soffit meets the roof cannot be pushed up, it is properly secured.

**Before securing this area ensure that no animal is present inside the attic

Turning Vents

A turning vent is one that turns with the force of wind and expels air from the attic. This can be screened from the outside or inside the attic. To screen from the outside you must remove the nails at the base of the vent where it connects to the roof (do not remove the nails along the top of the base, it may cause shingles to break). Tilt the vent back, measure the exposed hole leading into the attic, cut the screen and slide it up under the vent and on the shingles so that the entire hole is covered. Place the vent back down and refasten the screws. Remember to use roof patch. You can use this technique with the other vents as well but it will not prevent birds from nesting in the vents.

REMOVING RACOONS
from the Attic, Chimney and Under the Deck

Raccoons do not build nests; instead they pick a few suitable den sights that are dark and secluded to sleep in during the day, leaving to forage for food at night. Depending on the time of year, they usually come out after dark and return just before light. Raccoons do not hibernate, and are normally active every night. Whether or not they leave for the night depends on conditions outside.

Females and males do not co-habitate. During mating season (January to April) you may hear excessive noises like running and fighting. This is normal mating habits. Once babies are born, no other male or female may enter the den or get close to the mother's young because, being omnivores, they may eat their own kind.

Raccoons will eat anything, but given the choice, fish and chicken are by far their favorites. Raccoons are territorial and will inhabit and protect a certain area. If removed, another raccoon will replace it quickly, so almost no area is void of raccoons. The amount of food and shelter will determine the size of their territory and the number of raccoons present.

> **quick fact**
>
> Racoons are normally found in the attic in the cooler months. In the hot months, the attic will be unbearabe and the racoons will seek a cooler den site.

Raccoon(s) in the attic

This is a very common problem that is faced by many. Raccoons are infamous for getting into areas where they don't belong, especially warm, dark places. First of all, TRAPS DO NOT SOLVE THE PROBLEM! The problem is not that specific raccoon, but the area where it is entering.

Raccoons are territorial. If you trap and relocate an animal it creates a void in the territory allowing another animal to move in. Also, the smell of the animal is now in your attic and will attract others, especially during mating season. Your main goal is not to catch the animal, but to chase it out and permanently seal up the entry area to keep it out. Once that raccoon is chased out, it will never want to visit your attic again.

There are a few things to keep in mind when dealing with raccoons:

- they are smart
- they are creatures of habit
- they are curious
- they carry fleas
- they do not make nice pets
- they may carry rabies

Everything that they touch should be washed or thrown away. A large percentage of raccoons carry a roundworm in their feces. The eggs can be on the fur of the animal, insulation, wood, or anything that it comes in contact with. If these eggs are ingested by humans they may become very sick, and in extreme cases, death has occurred!

If raccoons are left in an attic over a period of time, severe damage will occur. Keep in mind that raccoons are the size of a small to medium dog and they urinate and defecate about as frequently and in the same quantities. Over time, insulation and drywall (the ceiling) becomes saturated, causing discoloration (yellow spots), bad odor and sagging, resulting in the ceiling's collapse (and hopefully the raccoon does not come with it!)

Raccoons 14

There are several ways to remove a raccoon without ever seeing the animal:

STEP 1. STICK YOUR HEAD UP IN THE ATTIC AND LOOK AROUND.
That's it. Most of the time the raccoon will be hiding in the soffit or overhang and you won't even see it. To be sure, make lots of noise. By invading the raccoon's space, you will make it feel uncomfortable and it may leave.

Listen at night and you will probably hear the raccoon leaving like it does every night. The question is, did it come back in the morning? Listen the next night, and if you don't hear a sound, seal up the entry hole the next day. If the area is not sealed you can guarantee re-entry by that raccoon or another one. After sealing the hole (to be sure it is gone) put a tablespoon of peanut butter on bread and leave it in the attic by the hatch overnight. If you don't hear anything and the peanut butter is still there the next day, problem solved.

Make sure you buy some mothballs or strong smelling deodorant to put up in the attic to remove the smell. Mothballs are an effective deodorant after the animal is removed, but rarely aids in the removal process (as most myths would have you believe). It actually could become harmful to the animal if in a confined area. If the raccoon has been in there for more than a year, you may want to contact a local restoration company to come and remove the insulation and re-insulate.

STEP 2. IF THE FIRST STEP IS NOT SUCCESSFUL AND YOU'RE STILL HEARING NOISES THE SECOND NIGHT, OR IF THE PEANUT BUTTER IS GONE, YOU ARE WELL ON YOUR WAY TO THE NEXT STEP.
You have already locked the raccoon in the attic for one night. This will make it very uncomfortable for the raccoon, so open the hole and listen. Then leave the hole open overnight and close it the next day. The following night put another peanut butter test in the attic and listen again.

This procedure will work if babies are also present. It is important to leave the hole open all night because if there are babies, it will take the mother several trips to remove and relocate them all.

If you have repeated these steps a few times and it didn't work go to Plan B.

When small (not mobile) babies are present
This is what the professionals do first. It is by far the most physical, but it works.

These steps may not work if:
a) the weather is cold outside and the raccoon does not leave every night or
b) the mother racoon does not have another den site (not common).

IF THERE ARE BABIES, GET YOUR STEPLADDER, BECAUSE YOU'RE GOING UP TO GET THEM. First determine exactly where the babies are by their crying. Even if it takes 24 hours, wait until they cry on their own. DO NOT BANG ON THE CEILING as this will cause the mother to move them to a different location in the attic. Also, do not go into the attic to see where they are unless you are going straight up to get them. If you leave the attic without the babies the mother will put them in a spot that you'll never get to.

Once you know exactly where they are, get your dust mask (for the fiberglass insulation), a bright flashlight and something to carry the babies in. Prepare yourself under the attic hatch. Get your exact position where the babies are so you are looking in that direction when you enter. Be as quiet as possible when you enter the attic, but go as quickly as possible. You want to see the mother on the babies. Stay at the hatch and make lots of noise now that you are in the attic so that she leaves the babies quickly to run and hide.

The reason for the surprise is that if the mother gets a chance, she will grab one of the babies in her mouth and run. With the element of surprise, the mother may leave the attic so you may want to have someone outside quietly watching from the ground (not the roof) so they can come in and tell you when the raccoon is out, off the roof, and gone. Normally the raccoon will just go into the soffit or overhang and hide. This is your chance, so crawl or walk (depending on the size of your attic) toward the babies. The

QUICKTIP
While in the attic, be careful to step only on the wood joists and not the drywall.

IF THE RACCOON HAS BEEN IN THERE FOR MORE THAN A YEAR, YOU MAY WANT TO CONTACT A LOCAL FIRE RESTORATION COMPANY TO COME AND REMOVE THE INSULATION AND REINSULATE.

mother will be hiding, scared and will not move.

Take the babies and carefully place them into the carrying device and leave the attic. If it is very cold outside you can leave them in the attic by the attic hatch; there is a good chance that by disturbing the mother so much, she will grab the babies and relocate to her other den site. If it is warm outside, you can place them in a box on the roof outside so the mother has to leave the attic to get to the babies. She will then most likely relocate the babies to an alternative den site. If the babies are semi-mobile, make sure the box sides are high enough to contain them or place the box on the ground at the base of the house where the raccoon climbs up and down.

It is very important to keep everything quiet that night so there are no interruptions in the relocating process. If you have a dog, bring it in for the night. It is most important that the mother and babies are reunited. If the mother does not find her babies you can be sure that a portion of your roof and attic will be destroyed the next day.

There is a very small chance that the mother will re-enter the attic with the babies. If so, repeat plan B. If the babies are gone the next day, seal up the entry hole and listen carefully for the next couple of days. It may take more than one night for the raccoon to relocate all the babies so be patient. Keep in mind that a sick or rabid raccoon would not have babies nor enter your attic to live.

After the animal is gone, spray the soffit, wall and attic with window cleaner which contains ammonia to remove the smell. This will ensure that no other animals are attracted to this area.

When mobile babies or no babies are present.

Remove a piece of soffit large enough to allow the animals to leave, but small enough to make re-entry difficult. The best thing about this technique is that it works well for mobile babies and there is no contact required.

This is a method that is fairly simple, but it works well. If the animal is in the attic, it is able to gain entry to the soffit that runs the perimeter of your house. Usually it will spend most of its time in there depending on the time of year. Repeat step A from earlier, but now seal up all areas on the roof including the entry hole.

Once the soffit panel is removed, leave it off overnight. Put some peanut butter on the wall 2-3 feet below the hole, to lure the raccoon out. It is important once the animal is gone to replace the soffit. If left off too long, the raccoon will begin to use the hole by swinging over the eaves and back in.

Now walk around your house and look for an area around the soffit that is just flat wall, with no windows, wires, or anything that a raccoon can grab on to. Place your ladder on the side of the house reaching up to the soffit. This should only be attempted on a lower soffit (7–10 feet from the ground)

quickfact | Racoons are very intelligent animals, so they will not turn to fight. Instead, they will run because you are four times their size.

A Raccoon in the Chimney

The number one mistake is to think that you can smoke out an animal. This action will only result in harm or death to the animal and they are much easier to remove when alive. Keep in mind that the only animal that can climb out is an adult raccoon. All other animals would be unable to get out through the top of the chimney.

This is one of the easier areas from which to remove raccoons because they are in a confined place and are afraid of humans. The reason raccoons are attracted to chimneys are:

a) it has the same shape and feel as a hollow tree
b) in the colder months there is heat coming out of the house through the damper and up the chimney making a warm den (a heated hollow tree)
c) in the summer months, the chimney is a damp, dark, and cool place, unlike the attic (an air conditioned hollow tree)

This guide will provide you with a few easy ways to remove raccoons from the chimney but remember that you must check the chimney thoroughly above and behind the damper to ensure that there are no babies present after the adult is removed! Baby season is anywhere from March to July and nine times out of ten, if babies are present they are not old enough to climb out.

In the months from August to February there could be more than one adult raccoon in the chimney, so always check thoroughly.

The first and best way to remove a raccoon from the chimney is to

> **quick fact**
> Mothballs are an effective deodorant after the animal is removed, but rarely aids in the removal process.

purchase chimney cleaning flexible poles that screw together. They are usually about 4-5 feet in length and the thickness of a pen. Get someone to stand quietly outside on the ground in a position where they can see the top of the chimney. Tell them not to take their eyes off the chimney top until they see the raccoon come out, down off the roof onto the ground and run away.

You begin by starting in the fireplace. Most of the time, the raccoon will sleep right on the damper so make some noise in the fireplace first and don't be shy. You may hear some rustling, so begin to gently tap on the metal damper (with a hammer), increasing the noise with each hit. Slowly open the damper and shine your flashlight in. By this time, the raccoon should almost be to the top, if not out. Slowly put your flexible chimney cleaning pole up into the damper and make sure it goes up the chimney stack joining each pole until you poke the animal completely out.

Rattle the poles in the chimney as you connect them; the more noise the better. The person outside will need to see the animal come out because you won't know for sure from inside. Then check the chimney for babies or another raccoon and when all is clear, seal up the top with the proper cap (see page 8 – Sealing a chimney).

If another adult raccoon is present, repeat this step over again. You may want to remove the damper completely to get a better look. If so, most dampers lift up and off their hinges and pull out.

IF YOU TRAP AND RELOCATE AN ANIMAL IT CREATES A VOID IN THE TERRITORY ALLOWING ANOTHER ANIMAL TO MOVE IN.

IF BABIES ARE STILL PRESENT IN THE CHIMNEY AFTER YOU COMPLETE THESE STEPS, YOU HAVE A COUPLE OF OPTIONS

OPTION ONE

Put on some work gloves, remove the babies from the top of the damper, place them in a sturdy box on the roof (or at least as close to the chimney cap as possible) and make sure the cap you put on is tight (see page 8). The mother raccoon will come back looking for her babies that night if not sooner. If the babies are semi-mobile, make sure the box sides are high enough to contain the babies or place the box on the ground at the base of the house where the raccoon climbs up and down.

If she does not find her babies, she will either pull until that cap comes off, or she will rip a hole in your roof looking for her babies. She will not go away quietly. If the babies are right there, she will grab them one by one and take them to her other established den site forgetting about yours (if it is a long way away it could take more than one night).

Make sure there is no human or animal intervention to stop the mother raccoon from returning to the site. Everyone must stay inside after the chimney is capped and the babies are on the roof in the box. If the babies are abandoned by the mother, contact your local animal control agency.

Raccoon under the Deck or Shed

Keep in mind that raccoons are opportunistic animals and normally go under a deck that has been inhabited by another animal before (refer to Skunk Under the Deck or Shed). All the same techniques apply, but you don't have to worry about getting sprayed.

OPTION TWO

If the weather is cold outside and the babies are very small or you cannot reach the babies in the damper, chase out the mother and leave the babies in the chimney (with the hole open at the top) and close the damper.

There is a good chance that the mother will be back that night to get her babies and take them out one by one. There is also a small chance that she will come back to stay; in this case you can try these steps again.

If you do not have flexible poles or visability into the chimney, bang on the damper with a hammer and then open it slowly until it is wide open and leave it open. Make as much noise as possible. This will make the raccoon so uncomfortable that it will either leave immediately or later that night and not return. The chances of it coming into the home are slim, but there are no guarantees.

Recheck the chimney and listen for noises the next day and install the chimney cap. Always listen for a few days after the cap is installed to ensure that no animals have been locked in.

SKUNK
under the deck or shed

Skunks like places in the warmer months that are cooler and dark during the day. The deck or shed (or any structure with no foundation) fits these requirements.

Skunks hate water, which can be a benefit when removing, as you will see. They have very poor vision, and rely mostly on their sense of smell (imagine that!) and hearing. These animals are typically misunderstood and are generally very peaceful, harmless animals that will only spray when startled or scared. Because they are slow, clumsy and curious they get into all sorts of trouble, either by entering a back yard with a dog or falling into someone's pool or window well. They cannot climb straight up although stairs or angled objects at 45 degrees or less are no problem. Skunks usually spray when in distress (unless they are babies trying out their new skill).

Just because you smell skunk does not mean you have a problem. It's not uncommon for a curious skunk to enter another skunk's den site or worse, entering a raccoon's den site. Let the spraying begin. Babies are normally present from May to July.

THE FOLLOWING TECHNIQUES WILL ALSO WORK WITH OTHER ANIMALS THAT LIVE UNDER STRUCTURES, INCLUDING RACCOONS, POSSUMS AND FOXES.

The most permanent way of keeping an animal from entering under a structure and ensuring that it is gone is by digging a small trench around the entire perimeter about 8-10 inches down and about 12-18 inches out. Skunks are excellent diggers, so if the soil is soft (i.e. sand) dig down further, and if the soil is hard (i.e. clay) go down as far as you can. (refer to step-by-step diagram on the next page). Make sure the trench is square. Once it is completely finished, measure the distance from the bottom of the trench to the bottom edge of the structure and extend the measurement onto the area of the deck or shed that the screen will be fastened to (1-2 inches). Measure the width of the trench (from the structure out.) and subtract two inches from the measurement. That will be the width of the screen (record both measurements). Cut and bend the screen (suggested in the materials section) into an L shape to fit the trench. The screen should fit down the back of the trench closest to the structure and come out and end in the deep part of the trench, making sure that there is a sharp 90 degree angle in the screen.

Overlap each piece of screen for easy connection along the trench. Use speedy ties for connecting the screen together.

Secure the screen to the deck or shed (with the recommended screws and washers) 12-18 inches apart horizontally around the perimeter. Fill in the dirt. The reasoning behind this technique is that the animal will butt its head up against the screen or structure and start digging, once it comes to the L bend there is nowhere to go. The animal is not smart enough to dig away from the deck or shed and will give up.

Make sure to check on the structure the next day after the screening is complete to ensure that no animal is locked in. If this were the case, you would see internal digging (behind the screen). A good test is to put one sardine under the structure (behind the screen) visible from the outside. If the food is not eaten the next day, everything should been fine. If there is digging or the food is gone, cut a hole in the screen 5" x 5". This will allow the animal to leave that night. The next day, return to seal up the hole with remaining screen from the job. Repeat the test to make sure the animal is gone. Keep in mind that baby skunks are born in May. You will want to complete this work between August and April.

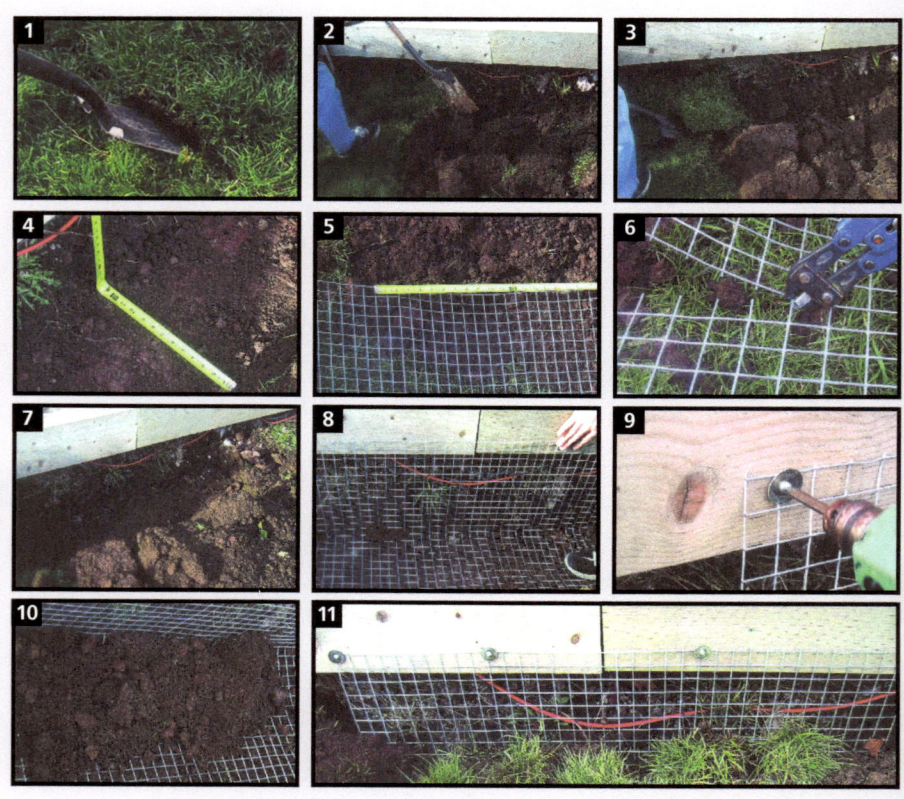

1. Dig a trench around the deck or shed.
2. Dig about 8 – 10 inches deep.
3. Make it 12 – 18 inches wide.
4. Measure your final width + depth.
5. Measure your screen.
6. Cut your screen to size.
7. Bend screen to required shape
8. Fit into the trench.
9. Secure screen every 12 inches.
10. Fill in the trench with the removed dirt.
11. Leave a food test visable behind the screen.

other options

If that sounds like too much work, and you are just looking for a TEMPORARY SOLUTION, or you need good suggestions on removing the skunk before sealing the area, here are some tips to try:

1. Skunks hate to get wet, so take your hose and give the deck a spray down with water, not too much, just enough to make it feel cold and damp. That should be enough to drive it away that night. Do not flood the area as baby skunks may be present and unable to get out.

2. Another thing to try is increasing activity on the deck. The skunk will not come out but will be so annoyed that it will surely leave after a few days of not sleeping.

3. The brave soul may try (if your deck is screwed down) removing a few deck boards close to where you think it sleeps (normally close to the house). This is almost guaranteed to make the skunk leave that night, if not that second. Be careful not to get sprayed!

4. Remove any food source (ie: composter, bird feeders, etc.). This may be an incentive for the animal to search for food in a different neighbourhood.

5. One last thing to try is putting urine around the perimeter of the deck. This will sometimes works.

Remember that all these tips are only temporary. You can be sure that either that skunk or another animal will be back to inhabit this great location if it is not sealed.

Removing **SQUIRRELS** from your house and attic

Squirrels are one of the most difficult animals to remove. The reason is that they rely more on instinct than intelligence. If you scare a squirrel out of its nest it will be back that day, and if you approach a squirrel it does not realize the size difference and may approach rather than retreat.

Grey squirrels may have two sets of litters, one in the spring (end of March to beginning of June) and the second in the summer (July to September) and average about 4-5 young per litter.

Squirrels are known for their chewing. If they're present in your attic they will be doing damage. It's only a matter of time before they cause some sort of structural damage. Follow these easy steps to ensure that the squirrels leave; and more importantly do not come back.

If possible, I strongly recommend removing the squirrel before the babies arrive. If babies are present, it will take 12 to 14 weeks until they are old enough to leave on their own. They may all leave or only one may remain.

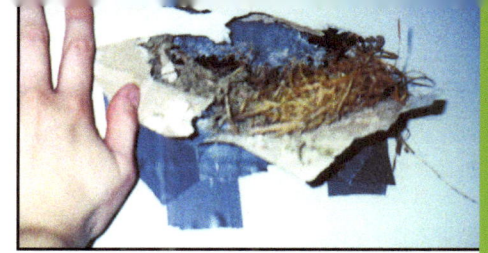

Damage to drywall caused by several playing and chewing squirrels

Squirrel in the house

This normally happens when a squirrel either decides to sit on the top of the chimney to keep warm or is looking for a new home and falls down the chimney. Squirrels cannot climb the inside of chimneys with a clay liner so they fall to the bottom and are either trapped above the damper, in your fireplace or come out the furnace into the basement. What to do? If the squirrel is trapped above the damper, the best and safest way to handle the situation is to open the flu at least 3-4 inches, which will allow the squirrel to enter the living space. It will probably not come out right away and may growl a bit. Close all the doors leading to different rooms so that it is confined to as small an area as possible. Then open a window or door (remove the screen) placing a blob of peanut butter on the ledge of the window or door and leave the room for as long as possible. The squirrel will make its way out if left alone and there is no noise.

If it is nighttime, make sure all the lights are on so the squirrel thinks that it is daytime and will stay active.

If you want to be sure that the animal has left, sprinkle flour or baking soda around the open area to the outside. This will allow you to see footprints if the squirrel has left. Do not chase the squirrel out, as you will only scare the squirrel and it will run the opposite way or end up breaking something.

The other approach is to rent or buy a live trap. If the squirrel is somewhere in the house and you have an approximate idea of where it is, set the live trap (use peanut butter as bait) and place it in an area where no one will disturb it. A light should be left on at all times.

The room with the trap must be totally quiet, as the squirrel is already stressed and any little noise will make it stay in the smallest space possible. This approach works well if the squirrel is in the basement where there are many places to hide and no way for it to escape.

Do not use traps in the attic. Only use them where you are able to check them a few times a day. If you catch a squirrel in the trap make sure to release it in your yard. First of all, they may have young close by that they have to get back to. Secondly, squirrels are territorial so if you trap and relocate any animal you create a void in that space allowing a new, potentially sick or diseased squirrel into your neighborhood. A new one will appear within approximately a month.

Squirrels: Are Babies Present?

There are a few ways of telling if a squirrel has had its babies:
1. Look for bare patches on its belly. This is where the babies will be feeding.
2. If there were two squirrels before and now there is just one. Most females will chase the male out when the babies are born because the male will normally eat them.
3. If there is increased activity. The squirrel must now feed several times a day and cannot stay out all day long like before. Once the babies begin to grow, it will go from one lone squirrel in the attic to several playing and chewing everything in sight! Having squirrels in your attic can cause serious damage so if this guide cannot help you, call a professional.

quick fact

Red squirrels are extremely territorial. The mating pair will spend most of their time outside collecting cones off the coniforous trees.

Getting to know your squirrels

It is important to determine what type of squirrel you are dealing with. This will determine active times and also points of entry.

Grey squirrels make a crying noise that sounds like a sick duck.

The grey squirrel is commonly found in urban settings. They can be grey, black and even brown but they are all one family of grey squirrels. Grey squirrels are typically active during the day.

The grey squirrel stores their food outside in the ground and they do not bring it into the attic or den site.

Red squirrels are mostly associated with coniferous trees (evergreens). They are extremely territorial and make a shrilling or chattering noise that can last for 5 seconds or more.

They are a smaller than a grey squirrel and a little bigger than a chipmunk which allows them access to the smallest of spaces.

The red squirrel may store their food in the attic, which sometimes sounds like rocks rolling around or dropping down walls. They may also be active at night.

IT IS VERY IMPORTANT NOT TO INTERFERE WITH THE SQUIRREL WHILE RELOCATION IS IN PROGRESS. ALLOWING THE SQUIRREL TO OPERATE NATURALLY WILL MAKE THE PROCESS THAT MUCH FASTER.

Squirrels in the attic

Squirrels are one of the most difficult animals to keep out once they have entered an attic. Once their scent is in the attic, it is embedded into the insulation and come next breeding season a squirrel will want in. They are such strong chewers that they can easily chew through wood, plastic and even metal.

Whatever you do, make sure that the entry area is sealed with the proper material outlined. If you're dealing with Red squirrels; move! All kidding aside, they are the hardest species to deal with, being smaller and more persistent than the Grey squirrel. Also, Red squirrels are known for entering at ground or roof level, whereas greys almost always enter at roof level. With red squirrels you have to start at the bottom of the exterior and work up.

To determine the entry point, start by following movements in the attic. They are most active in the early morning and evening. Usually where the noise stops is the exit and entry point (typically there is more than one). To determine the entry area(s) you are going to have to listen carefully for a few days and if possible, put a ladder up to the roof to have a look around. Normally squirrels make their nests close to the entry area (a good place to start). Depending on the time of year, you may have to go into the attic. Between April and September there may be babies present.

When you have located the hole(s) and there is a chance of babies, go up into the attic to look around. You'll need a stepladder, a dust mask for the insulation, a flashlight and a small box (a Kleenex box works well). Once into the attic, head for the entry hole. This is where the nest is likely located. The nest will look like a mound of insulation, and you will have to carefully search through the insulation to check for babies. If no babies are found you can leave the attic and go to installing an exit door.

QUICK TIP

If you are certain that no babies are present, there is a device on the market that will allow the squirrel to leave but not get back in. If you search the web, type in "squirrel one way doors".

If you find babies and it is warm outside, carefully place them in the box and take them out of the attic. Once outside, place the box with the babies on the roof and leave the entry hole open. The mother will hear the babies crying on the roof and exit the attic. She will feel very uncomfortable and most likely move her young to a different den site. Do not interfere with her while on the roof. If she goes back in you may have to repeat the steps.

There is a chance that the squirrel had left the attic while you were inside. If you have checked the attic and no babies are present and you are quite sure the adult is not present, seal up the holes. Make sure that you listen for the next couple of days.

You can place peanut butter inside the attic visible from the hatch as a food test. Check the sealed hole and food the next day. If the food is gone or internal chewing is present there may be a squirrel still in, so open the hole for a day and repeat the steps. If the hole is not disturbed and the food is not touched, job done.

If you are not willing or unable to enter the attic (too small of an area) there is another way.

Seal all areas including the entry hole when there is no noise (middle of the day is best). When the squirrel returns to get back in it will chew (more in the winter than in the summer). It's normal for the squirrel to chew but if the squirrel is frantically chewing and crying for hours, there are probably babies still inside.

So open the hole and allow the mother to enter the attic and stand out of sight. By being locked away from her babies, that squirrel is stressed and will probably go back in, grab the babies one by one and relocate them to another den site. Once the squirrel has taken the last baby and has not returned to the attic for a few hours, seal up the hole. Make sure not to interfere with the relocation process. Remember that litter sizes can range up to 10 babies.

Worst case scenario is that the squirrel goes back in after you open the hole and will not come back out. In this case leave the hole open for a full day and see what happens (it may take that squirrel longer to relocate). Repeat the steps. This will work, it just may take a little longer.

It is very important not to interfere with the squirrel while relocation is in progress. Allowing the squirrel to operate naturally will make the process that much faster.

BIRDS
in the house or vents

This is a very common occurrence in new homes: birds arrive home from the south after the winter to discover a house on their feeding field, or in an area where they once foraged for food. They then find the wall vent (with little flaps for protection from the elements) is a perfect, dark and dry place to raise a family. European starlings (Sturnus Vulgaris) are the most common species of bird to inhabit a wall vent. They are not native to North America, and displace many native birds' nesting areas. Birds will begin to gather nests in early spring and will have their young in June or July.

If the nest and birds remain in your vent for a period of time you will experience bird mites entering into your home and in the summer months a foul smell will be present. Also, the nest will block the vent allowing no ventalation from these areas.

Bird in the House

This normally happens in the same way a squirrel enters the living space; they sit on top of the chimney and fall in while exploring. Once down too far, the bird cannot fly directly up and is trapped at the bottom, finding its way out of the furnace (if attached) or the fireplace into your house.

The best way to remove the bird is to close all the curtains and blinds in the house making it as dark as possible. Open a door or window (remove the screens) allowing light to come from that one spot only. Birds are attracted to light and will fly directly toward it. Do not chase or scare the bird. Leave it alone and it will find its own way out in a matter of minutes. If you try to help or guide it out you will only scare and confuse the bird which can lead to injury and/or damage to your home. If the bird is on the damper of the fireplace, open it and repeat the steps above. This will allow the bird to exit the fireplace on its own and exit. If you can hear noises and you're not sure where the bird is, check the cleanout. All fireplaces and flus have a small opening (covered with a metal plate) usually at the bottom of the chimney in the basement that allows you to clean the ashes out. Check this area because animals can access this as well. If a bird is in this area you can get a glove and reach in and remove the bird or if you prefer, open the hole and repeat the previous steps.

Birds in the Vent

Materials needed:
- flashlight
- coat hanger wire

(you may need to add some tools as the job gets more complicated)

Most owners of new homes will experience this at some point.

Start by checking and watching your vents (before the birds have babies, the nest will be small). From inside, tap on the inside fan and turn the fan on to see if there is airflow on the outside. Check with a flashlight from the outside to see if the vent is all clear. If yes, go to sealing up the vent, if not, continue.

If the bird has already had its babies, then you can take the easy route, grin and bear it for two months and they will all leave when they are big enough to fly instead of taking on the task of removing them (which could be tough).

Removing Mom, Babies and the Nest from the Wall Vent.

First, have someone stand outside watching the vent while you go inside to the vent that is the problem. Tap on the vent itself to make sure there are no birds in the fan unit (this may also scare the mother out) then proceed to turn the fan on. This will push some of the nesting material toward the outside (also scaring any birds in the vent tube).

If you see nesting material in the inside vent cover, remove the vent cover and fan first, then go to the outside of the house to the vent. Take a flashlight and a coat hanger wire (undone and straightened except for the hook on the end). Remove the flaps of the vent carefully (they are usually slotted). This will allow you to look directly into the vent with the flashlight to see what is present (make sure you wear eye protection). If you are dealing with a hood vent, you are going to have to completely remove it. The objective is to slowly feed the wire in with the hook end first, past the nest. Then rotate the wire, hopefully hooking onto the nest, and pull it out all in one clump (babies and all). This is normally an easy procedure if the nest is close, the babies very young and the vent is metal and straight.

This job can be nearly impossible if the nest is far in, the babies are mobile or the tube is corrugated plastic. If the babies and nest come out easily, go to the next step: sealing up the hole.

Be patient when removing birds as they are of a low intelligence. It may take a little longer for them to exit in the right direction.

IF YOU ARE HAVING TROUBLE LET'S GO THROUGH SOME ALTERNATE STEPS:

First, if the nest is too far in, you can buy longer wire (at any hardware store). Or remove the fan from inside so it is an 'open' hole and buy chimney cleaning rods. They usually come in four foot lengths that screw together. Push the nest from the outside, to the inside fan and remove the nest from there. Also try this if the

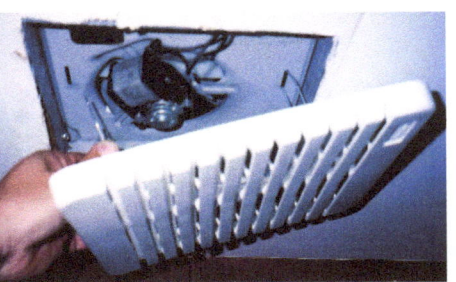
Typical indoor bathroom vent

babies are mobile. Make sure (if possible) to close the door to contain the birds.

If the pipe is corrugated plastic there are two options. One is to attach window screen on the end of your vacuum cleaner hose with elastics and feed the hose into the pipe until it reaches the nest and each bird, slowly pulling each one out. Extensions for your hose are available at hardware and vacuum stores. This will ensure a clean vent. If the vacuum is not an option, the vent liner can usually be pulled right out from the outside. From the inside, remove the fan and the housing and seal the inside end of the pipe with duct tape. Then from the outside pull the pipe slowly out until it is completely removed from the house and remove the birds from the pipe. To replace the pipe, buy the proper length from a hardware store (it's cheap) and feed it in from the outside attaching both ends.

Make sure never to lock birds in. If a bird dies in the vent there will be a terrible smell for about 2 months, maggots will appear resulting in having to cut a hole in the ceiling to remove the dead birds. If the birds have made a hole in the corrugated pipe and are living in the joist space, you are going to have to leave them until the birds leave on their own. You can then proceed to seal the hole.

Keeping the family together

If the babies are not mobile place them in a jug (a 2 litre plastic pop bottle works well). Start by cutting a 3"x 3" hole in the side of the jug, and this will keep them out of the elements attach it to the side of your home or on the vent. Put some of the nesting material in the bottom of the jug and place the birds on top of their new nest. This is to allow the mother to return to the vent and feed the birds until they are big enough to leave. When the birds are gone, remove the nesting device, a job well done! Remember to make sure the vent is sealed properly before putting up the nesting jug.

Bird in the Walls

Another common occurrence is when birds nesting in the attic or wall vent rattle or push something loose. This allows the bird access to the wall. If they fall down between the studs, they may be unable to get out. In this case, the only way to remove them is to cut a small hole in the wall with a drywall saw. Make it large enough to get your hand in (it has to be repaired anyway). Make sure you determine the exact location before cutting (this is not easy). The bird is normally found in the wall at floor level. If left, the bird will die and the decaying smell will remain for up to 2 months.

The most common birds that invade wall vents are European Starlings, which are not native to North America. Birds do not have a sense of smell. It is permissible to handle young birds for short periods of time. The mother will not detect human scent and reject her young contrary to popular myths.

sealing the vent

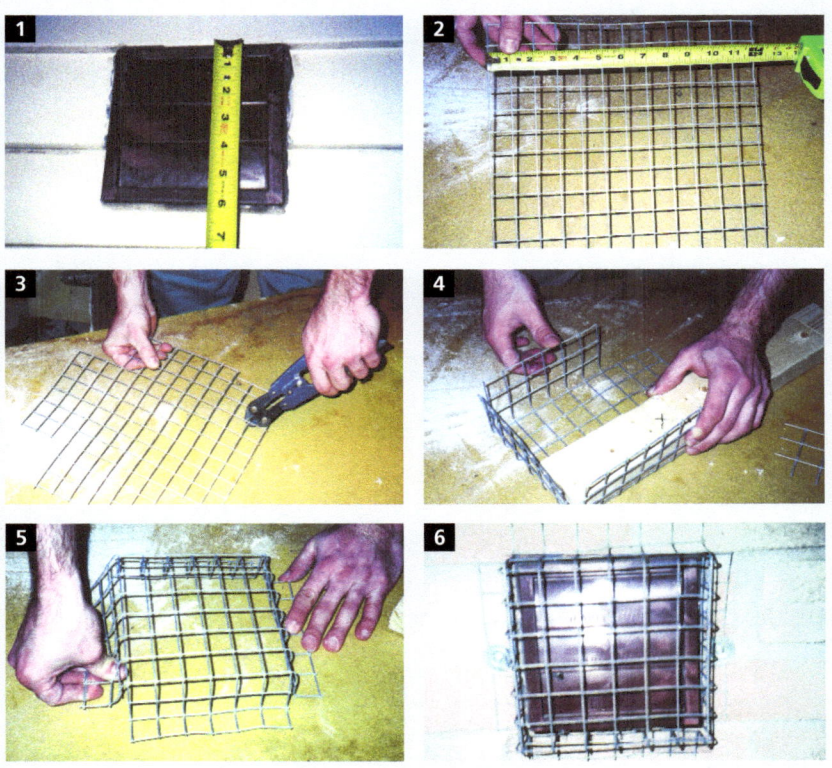

1. Measure the height and width of vent.
2. Measure your screen.
3. Add 3" to your height and width measurement and cut 3" squares out of corners.
4. Bend sides up creating a square bowl.
5. Bend the edges out to create a 1" lip which will fit against the wall (the 2" height is to let the vent's flaps open).
6. Secure to the wall with screws and washers.

HOW TO

replace a
damaged wall vent

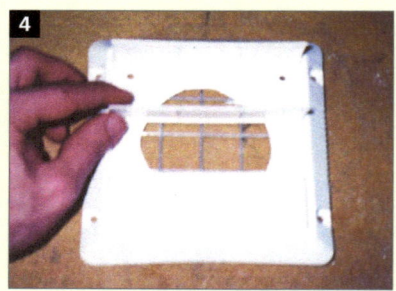

❶ Remove louvres from your new vent carefully.

❷ Cut off any raised lips with tin snips or knife to make the vent as flat as possible.

❸ Cut a piece of screen to fit into the back of the vent (usually 4" x 4"). Place screen on back of vent, adhering with dabs of silicone. Let dry.

❹ Replace louvres on the front of the vent. Attach to the wall with screws.

Sealing the Vent

Materials Needed
- Screen
- Cutters
- Drill, Drill bit and screws

You may need to use some additional tools.

If your existing louvered vent is still in good shape, there is no need to replace it. You can create a box out of screen and attach it with screws and washers. First measure the length and width of the vent and add 6 inches to each measurement. Cut the screen to the desired size and cut out 3 inches at each corner. Bend the flaps in to create a square bowl and then bend the last one inch out the opposite way, resulting in a bird proof box that will easily screw over the vent (see diagram on page 38).

Replacing a Damaged Wall Vent

If the vent is damaged here's what to do. First begin by making sure you have the right vent. The plastic vents with the three or four flaps are the easiest to install and they come in different colours too. If you have a metal hood vent, even better. Some hardware stores even offer bird-proof vents.

For the plastic louvered vent, remove any bits on the wall left by the old vent or remove the existing damaged vent. Facing the back of the new vent, first cut the small lip off making a flat surface. Measure the inside and cut a piece of screen to fit flat inside (usually 4"x 4" or 6"x 6"), put a dab of silicon connecting the steel to the plastic, and let dry for 15 minutes. Place the vent on the wall over the hole with the louvers facing down in the closed position. Screw the vent into the wall in the holes provided (if drilling into brick, pre-drill holes and use plugs), making sure the vent is straight. Add silicon around the perimeter of the vent where the vent meets the house, which prevents water from entering. You should be able to lift up one louvre and see the screening normally, when the fan is off, the louvers will stay closed. Make sure you use the materials specified.

To screen a steel hood vent measure the length and width of the under, open part of the vent. Cut the screen, adding one inch to each side. Cut out one inch squares in each corner and bend three sides up one inch and the side against the wall bend down one inch. This should fit around the outside of the vent and can be attached with one screw and washer on each side.

Birds 40

Removing and Excluding
BATS from your House and Attic

Bats are nocturnal. Their diet consists mostly of flying insects. They have very poor vision and rely on sonar, which allows them to detect objects while flying. There are many species of bats, the most common in North America being the Big and Little Brown Bat (Eptesicus Fuseus). Both species are similar; the Big Brown Bat is the size of a large mouse. Bats are by far the easiest species to deal with. Experts say that if you get one in the house it usually means that you have 30 in the attic, 2 means 60, and so on. It's pretty scary when a bat is flying around your bedroom at 2:00 am but remember that it is just looking for a way to get out.

Bats are beneficial to have around as they consume 1/2 of their body weight in insects each night. After removing the bats (or before) you may want to install a bat house. Position it in a nearby tree as high as possible and facing south. Female bats have 1-2 young per year.

quickfact Bats only enter a living space by mistake so make it as easy as possible for them to leave. They are just looking for a way out.

Bats in the House

A bat usually enters the living space from the attic; very rarely will it fly in through an open window or door. This usually happens between July and the end of August. The reason is that baby bats were born in your attic and are finally becoming mature and able to leave in search of food. They leave in the evening, feed and return before dawn. Instead of coming out of the attic to the outside they accidentally go down between the interior and exterior wall of your house until they reach the basement (or an opening) and this is where they come out and start flying around looking for a way out. Bats instinctively circle in the air until they find an opening, traveling in an upward motion. If they do not find an opening in the basement they will squeeze under the basement door coming upstairs and begin looking again until they reach the top level. They are usually so exhausted (with no food) by this time that they will stop and hide. A bat can go into what is called a torpor state in which they lower their heart rate and can live (depending on the weather) anywhere from one week upto 8 months. Over 90% of homeowners find out they have bats only when one enters the house and wakes them up in the middle of the night.

Bats in winter

Little Brown Bats migrate during the cold winter months whereas Big Brown Bats are known to hibernate for the winter. You probably won't see them in your attic but they might be there.

Removing a bat from inside the house:

1. REMAIN CALM. If the bat is flying around in a room where you can shut the door and you do not want to deal with the bat, open the window and remove the screen, close the door behind you and stuff a towel under the crack of the door.

If the bat flies around again anytime that night it will find the open window and leave, guaranteed. Check in the morning and it should be gone.

Do not encourage the bat to fly. It will only confuse it even more and will make the process longer.

2. THIS IS HOW THE PROFESSIONALS DO IT. Wait until the bat has landed and you're feeling courageous. Let the bat sit for at least 2-5 minutes. It will slow down and not move when you approach it. Remember that their mouths are normally too small to fit around your pinkie finger but they do have teeth!

Get a jar with a lid (empty peanut butter jars work best.) Slowly approach the bat, place the jar over it and with the lid, flick it in. Take it outside to release it. You may have to gently shake the bat out of the jar. If the bat begins to fly before putting the jar over it repeat step 2.

REMEMBER THAT BATS ARE HARMLESS AND JUST WANT TO GET OUT. USE GLOVES TO PREVENT CONTACT AS THEY DO CARRY DISEASES LIKE RABIES (THEY ALSO MAY HAVE FLEAS)

The benefits of a bat house

You may also want to install a bat house NOT on your house, but near it, in a tree. It should be on the south east side of the tree and as high as possible. Having more bats around your home means less flying insects to deal with!

All the plans and instructions to build a bat house are easily found on the internet.

Removing Bats from your Attic

This is easier than you think, and you don't have to come into contact with any bats.

First, go outside just before it starts to get dark and take a walk around your house looking for droppings on the ground or walls. The droppings are similar to mice droppings (about the size of a grain of rice) but if you rub a piece between your fingers it will crumble into dust whereas mice droppings are hard and will squish.

Most of the time bats will enter where the outside wall meets the soffit or overhang of the house. Bats enter by landing on the wall and crawl up squeezing into any gaps they can find. Keep walking around your house; if it's a typical summer night you will hear or see them come out. If you don't see anything the first night, keep trying until you see at least one come out or have a good idea of the entry hole location.

The first thing you must do is construct a bat cone. This allows the bat to leave but not to get back in. (See Installing an exit door.)

Remember that you can only remove bats the last week of July to the first week of September because this is when the babies will be big enough to leave on their own.

In order to make sure that the bats will not gain entry again, you must seal up all the areas where the bats may be able to get in. That means any gap you see should be caulked, even if you think it is too small for a bat. If the bats are entering in an area where the wall meets the soffit or where there is a gap smaller than one inch, silicon can be used.

Measure roughly how much you will need and (the smaller the gap the less you will have to use) buy something with a 30 year+ guarantee so you won't have to repeat the job in five years. Caulking comes in all colours so take your pick (if unsure use clear). You will need a ladder and caulking gun to apply the caulking in every place that there is a crack. The reason we use caulking is that it's pliable, and as your house settles over the years, the caulking will shift and expand with it.

> **quick fact**
> You will never see a bat in the attic as they are too small and will hide in small areas inaccessable to humans.

If there are areas that are larger than one inch, use screening called hardware cloth (the same stuff the bat cone is made of). It is steel screening 0.5"x 0.5" or smaller, which is just small enough to keep bats out. This screen can be cut with mini bolt cutters or tinsnips and fastened with screws and washers or staples. The screen is a little tricky to use so apply silicon wherever possible.

Once you have sealed all the areas other than the entry hole, install the bat cone (see creating a bat exit door) over the hole securing it with screws and washers and filling in any gaps where the house meets the cone with silicon. The silicon, when dry, will just pull off so you don't have to be neat. Make sure the large end of the cone is attached to the house. You can leave the door on as long as you want but it should be there for a minimum of one week. You may want to walk around the house the first night just to ensure that the door is functional and the bats are able to get out.

After a week or so, if you are convinced all the bats are out, remove the door and seal up the hole. Keep in mind that bats can fit into the smallest of holes so you may want to re-inspect the house the following spring just to be sure. Remember to inspect all areas of your house, because even if the area where the soffit meets the wall is the most common entry point, there are plenty of other areas that a bat will find. (See Areas Vulnerable to Wildlife)

Hardware Cloth

Bat exit door

This is an extremely easy and inexpensive device to make using hardware cloth either 1/2" x 1/2" or smaller and a set of tinsnips. Start by measuring and cutting a piece of screen about 9" in width

creating
an exit door
(or "one-way" door)

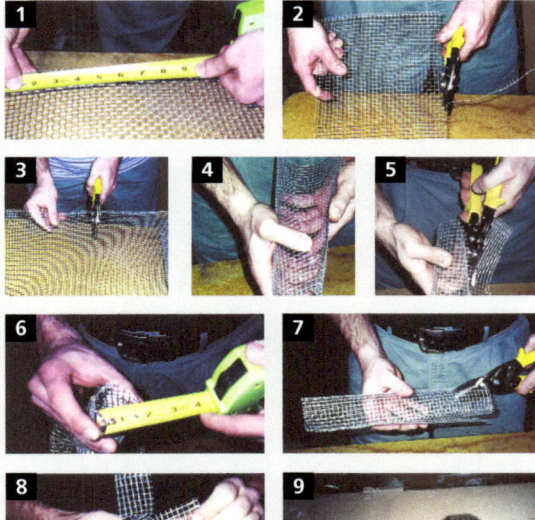

1. Measure out 9" x 18" on the screen.
2. Cut screen to size.
3. Keep the prongs (ends of screen) on.
4. Roll into cone shape.
5. Cut off excess screen.
6. The small end should be no less than 1" in diameter.
7. Cut larger end into four sections.
8. Flare out sections on large end.
9. Attach large end with screws and washers to bat exit area.

and 18" in length. Take the piece of screen and roll it into a cone shape, with one end just touching (diameter 9") and the other end smaller, leaving the small hole about 1-2" in width. Bend a few of the screen prongs over to secure the cones position and trim off the excess screen. Now that the screen is in a cone shape, cut into the large end 3-4 inches in four places and flare out the sides. You have now created an exit door for bats that is ready for installation. This door should fit into almost any area. Make sure the small end is jetting out away from the house. Secure with screws and washers and fill in any gaps with silicone. The silicone will pull off easily when removing the door. Once the door is off, seal the hole with silicone or cover with screen. If that is too hard, just fold up the door tight so nothing can enter.

Removing and Controlling **MICE**

The general rule is that if you see one in the house or hear one in the attic there are at least ten more in the walls and ceiling. Mice are generally nocturnal, so the time to hear them is in the middle of the night chewing on drywall or wood in the wall or attic. It will sound very loud because the house is quiet and the vibration and echo of the object they are chewing is magnified. A good test to try while the chewing is in progress is banging with your fist on the area that you hear the noise. If it stops, or stops and then starts again, it's mice. If you hear it move around or scurry away it's definitely bigger than a mouse. The most popular time for mice to begin looking for a nice warm den is when it becomes cold outside. This is when activity will increase.

Some common food sources for mice are bird seed and composters. You may want to put these objects as far as possible from your house.

The same principles that relate to mice can be applied to rats. Mice have a life span of about 1 year. In that time they can have up to 12 litters averaging 4 to 5 young. Do the math!

Mice in the House

A few things that work: Mice cannot chew through steelwool, so take a walk around the outer perimeter of the house blocking any hole larger than a dime. Start with the garage, as clutter and garbage attracts most animals. They may already be living in your garage and over time they may find their way into the house. When you find a hole and it does not need airflow, put some steel wool in and pack it with a screw driver. Then put silicone or expanding foam over the steel-wool to keep it in place. Mice usually enter at ground level but have been known to climb straight up brick walls, so start at the bottom and work up.

It may be imposible to seal every area on the exterior of the house, so you may also want to use something inside the home. There are various methods inside the home that you can try, but keep in mind that whatever you use to control mice in the house, always put it where you have seen or heard the mice. Secondly, Keep it away from children and pets! If you set traps, make sure that you check them every day to ensure that the animal does not suffer and if you decided on poison, only use it in the attic or in the walls and floor. To get it into the floor you can remove a floor vent and move the air duct over just enough to drop the poison into the floor. The same goes with the walls. Remove the outlet cover and drop the packs down the wall into the joist space. For the attic you can stand at the hatch and throw the packs into the attic. Do this every six months to a year and it should keep the problem under control.

Mice like to build their nests around heating ducts where it is nice and warm. Remember that cats will eat mice and even if the poison is hidden in the wall or attic the cat may ingest a poisoned mouse and get sick. If you follow the easy steps above, your mice problems should scurry away.

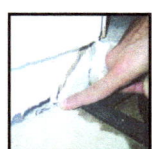  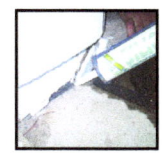  

Small cracks in the foundation or holes in exterior walls can be packed with steel wool and sealed with silicon

Other
NUISANCE wildlife

To be clear, wildlife should not be considered nuisance, but having a squirrel dig up all the flower bulbs in the garden you just planted or your dog getting sprayed by a skunk once a week could become annoying.

This chapter shows you how to deal with some of these everyday encounters.
- animals in the garage/shed
- racoons in the yard
- squirrels in the garden
- skunks in your yard
- animals in the composter

Always keep in mind that these animals were here long before we were and will be around long after we're gone. The key is to try to live in harmony and respect their habitat. They need to eat, drink and sleep just like us.

> **quick fact**
> Some unfinished garages may have open joists on the walls and ceilings. Depending upon the construction of your home, this may allow an animal access to your attic.

Animal in the garage or shed

An animal in the garage is a very common occurrence, as most people keep garbage in their garage, which is a major attraction for most animals. Common animals that enter a garage are squirrels, skunks, raccoons and possums. If the garage door is left open a crack in the evening or throughout the night, it's not uncommon for an unwanted guest to wander in looking for food or shelter. Clutter, woodpiles, or anything an animal can crawl under for shelter is an attraction. The easiest way to remove an animal is to open the door and leave it open for a few hours. Make a little noise in the garage (not enough to startle and spray but disturb) and then LEAVE IT ALONE! That little disturbance is enough for it to leave. If there is junk or a place to hide you can do a few things. The first is to put a radio in the garage (set to a talk station) or try moving stuff around (if you dare).

If there are areas to hide in and you are unsure whether the animal has left after trying these tricks, here is the sure-fire way to find out. Close the garage door and place a piece of bread with peanut butter on it in the middle of the floor. The next morning if it's gone, the animal is still present and it has been locked in for the night. Leave the garage door open (4 inches off the ground) the next night. Then close the door and repeat the peanut butter step the following night. Do this until the door is closed and the food has not been touched overnight. It may take longer, but it works and there is no physical contact.

How to control animals in the yard

Unfortunately there is little you can do to stop an animal from entering the yard. For each animal there are tips you can try – to make it less attractive to the animal.

RACCOONS

Raccoons will enter a yard for a few reasons:

1. It is their nightly pathway to a specific destination (raccoons will use the same route nightly).

2. There is accessible food i.e. birdseed, grapes, a fish pond, composter (all of these are attractions and if you are not willing to part with them you may have to grin and bear it).

A dog is a good deterrent but is not a guaranteed solution. Making food sources harder to get to may work. For a pond thief you can try placing a net over the pond and securing it with rocks or stakes. There are also motion detector sprinklers that can be installed for a suprise soaking.

SQUIRRELS IN THE GARDEN

One thing to try for keeping squirrels out of the garden is to spread human hair on the soil. Any local salon will be happy to donate some clippings.

SKUNKS

Skunks are a little easier to keep out if your yard is fenced, because they cannot climb. They are great diggers so inspect the perimeter of your yard for any holes, openings or bends in the fence and fix them.

The chapter on skunks under structures will also work around the perimeter of the yard, but it is a lot of work. An easier sloution may be to place gravel, rocks and stones around the perimeter of the fence, which will definitely deter them from digging.

quickfact Remember that the number one reason that an animal enters your yard is for food. Take that away, or at least make it difficult to access and the problem will slowly diminish.

ANIMALS IN THE COMPOSTER

Mice and rats are the most common animal found here. There are few products on the market that are environmentallly friendly and not harmful to the animal that can be purchased to deter them. Something else you can try is spreading cayan pepper into the composter. This should at least keep the animals out.

BIRDSEED, GRAPES, A FISH POND OR COMPOSTER MAY PROVIDE A RACOON WITH A REASON TO ENTER OR RE-ENTER YOUR YARD NIGHTLY

trapping

If you have to trap for whatever reason, use live traps. Catch the animal – you can bet that animal is scared – and release it in the same place that you caught it. You can be sure that it will not be back but will still remain in the area keeping other animals out of its territory.

The contents, instructions and information in this book are based solely on the authors experience in the wildlife removal field and are not guaranteed in any way to always work or be successful. Wild animals are unpredictable and their behaviour can not be predicted. Approach and proceed with caution and common sense when dealing with all forms of wildlife. The materials used and installation/building practises in protecting and preventing animal entry is solely based on the authors experience and is not guaranteed in any way. Always use caution and safety guidelines when using any and all equipment and material, follow the manufactures' instructions carefully to avoid injury.

www.ingramcontent.com/pod-product-compliance
Lightning Source LLC
LaVergne TN
LVHW010019070426
835507LV00001B/10